CYRA-NOSE
the SEA ELEPHANT

by Lou Jacobs, Jr.
illustrated with photographs

AN ELK GROVE BOOK

 CHILDRENS PRESS, CHICAGO

Acknowledgement

The author wishes to thank the Public Relations office and photographer Bob Noble at Marineland of the Pacific for making so many fine photographs available; and John Prescott, Curator of Mammals at Marineland, who so aptly described the capture and training of sea elephants to insure the accuracy of this story. My thanks also to my wife Barbara Jacobs who took some of the photographs with me.

Library of Congress Cataloging in Publication Data

Jacobs, Lou.
  Cyra-nose, the sea elephant.

  SUMMARY: Describes the life of an elephant seal on a Pacific island and his ultimate capture and new life at Los Angeles' Marineland.

  "An Elk Grove book."

  1. Northern elephant seal—Juvenile literature.
[1. Northern elephant seal.   2. Seals (Animals)]
I. Title.
QL737.P64J32   599′ .748   72-10185
ISBN 0-516-07621-3

j599. 7
J

1 2 3 4 5 6 7 8 9 10 11 12 13 14 15 16 17 18 19 20 21 22 23 24 25 R 75 74 73

CYRA-NOSE
the SEA ELEPHANT

This is Cyra-nose (say Sear-a-nose). If you were a *sea elephant,* you'd think he was a handsome guy. His beautiful nose curls out as long as an elephant's trunk. For a sea elephant, he's about the right size, around 3,500 pounds of skin and *blubber.* Blubber is fat which keeps sea animals warm in freezing ocean water.

Cyra-nose is 14 feet long, and if he wore a belt, it would stretch nine feet. You can almost hear his loud snort that sounds like a broken foghorn.

About eight years ago Cyra-nose was just a baby, called a *pup* or a *calf.* He was born on Guadalupe Island in the Pacific Ocean off the coast of Mexico. That's where thousands of sea elephants go every winter to find mates and have their babies.

A long time ago the sailors who passed Guadalupe Island saw these huge animals, and named them sea elephants. They are also called *elephant seals,* the largest members of the seal family.

Cyra-nose is a male called a *bull*. These mother animals are called *cows*, but they're not like any cows you'll find on a dairy farm. Cows stay very close to each other on the beach to protect their calves. Lady sea elephants look more like other seals because they have short, pretty noses. Imagine the noise on this beach as the snorting and barking mothers *nurse* their squealing pups.

Not many zoos have elephant seals, because Mexico allows only a few to be captured. How do you capture a ton of blubber, anyway? You'll see.

Cyra-nose might not have grown so big if he had been born about 80 years ago. Hunters had killed nearly all the animals on Guadalupe by 1892. They wanted the thick layer of blubber under the sea elephant's skin to make oil to burn in lamps. Didn't anyone care enough to save these unusual animals from disappearing?

Yes, Mexico sent soldiers to Guadalupe to protect the elephant seals. New babies were born and families grew. Now thousands of fat cows, bulls and calves live on Guadalupe's beaches during the winter.

Cyra-nose sleeps here with one of his families. When many cows mate with a bull, they are called his *harem*. Cyra-nose sometimes fights other bulls to protect his harem.

The pups are only a week old, but each weighs more than 50 pounds.

As a little calf, like this one, Cyra-nose stayed close to his mother. He took milk from her for almost a month until he grew to be a 300-pound butter-ball. His mother was very fat when her pup was born. While she nursed Cyra-nose, she lost weight, but might have made only one trip to the ocean for food. It's lucky Mom doesn't get very hungry. If she were away, some careless bull might crush the young pup.

When Cyra-nose was about a month old, he tried to swim. At first he just played in the low waves. As he became stronger, he went into deeper water with his mother and other pups. Finally, one day when Cyra-nose could find his own fish in the sea, he left Guadalupe to see the great Pacific Ocean. The next winter when he returned to the island, he probably didn't even know his own mother.

Eight years later Cyra-nose has grown to be a big, fat bull. After his morning nap one day, he sees some strange new animals. They have legs instead of *flippers,* and they've come to this island in a big wooden thing. The new animals in white shirts don't look dangerous, so Cyra-nose just watches them.

This sea elephant has never been afraid of anything, because he has big teeth and two short *tusks*. He can bite sharks or other animals that try to hurt him. He can even bite the leg of a funny animal in a white shirt, whatever it is.

In the ocean Cyra-nose can dive a thousand feet deep, and swim like a torpedo with fins. He can stay underwater at least eight minutes and come up a mile away from where he started.

But Cyra-nose can't move very fast on the beach. The two-legged animals walk right up to him with their big net. Whoops! The net falls over Cyra-nose! It feels very strange, and he wants to get away from those little animals all in a row.

Soon Cyra-nose is angry. How could he be caught in so much seaweed while lying on the beach? He tries to stand high and bite somebody, but he's tangled in the net. The men move a large hoop and pull on a rope. The net closes around Cyra-nose as though he were a big fish in the sea.

If he can get to the water, Cyra-nose knows he can swim away from the pesky animals in white shirts. But they twist the net behind him, and follow the big bull. There's no need to push or carry Cyra-nose. He moves along like a small war tank. He doesn't know he's helping the men capture him.

It's a tug of war! Cyra-nose strains forward and the men pull backwards. A cow and her pup can only watch Cyra-nose struggle in his big net suit. The men hook another rope to the net. The new rope runs all the way to a fishing boat in the harbor.

If Cyra-nose were free, he would certainly bite a few legs and scare away the little animals that are bothering him. But all he can do is struggle and bark loudly at them.

At the edge of the beach Cyra-nose makes his last try
to swim under the deep water. But the men pull the rope,
and he becomes a net full of sea elephant drawn along
like a fat trailer.

Cyra-nose has never been so close to a boat. He is moving through the water, but he can't swim. He can only use his flippers to stay afloat. Well, at least he's not being hurt.

Up, up and away! Cyra-nose flies low as the net is lifted above the fishing boat. Flying is so strange that Cyra-nose forgets to bark or snort. How would you like to fly through the air in a net when you'd rather be swimming like a torpedo?

What's this big box? Cyra-nose pokes his trunk over
the edge and looks around. The box doesn't feel like sand
or rocks, and it's not wet. He begins to relax after the
men find he weighs one and a half tons. He's more than
3,000 pounds of prize sea elephant—and still growing!

The net is gone! Cyra-nose feels free again—almost. He has no place to go, and the men put a top on his big cage. For the next two days Cyra-nose takes a boat ride to Los Angeles, California. All he can do is watch the ocean where he'd like to be.

The men in white shirts are collectors from Marineland of the Pacific, a sea zoo near Los Angeles. They have special permission to capture him and seven other elephant seals. Two are cows and six are bulls. One cow and one bull will later be sent on an airplane to the Mexico City Zoo.

Cyra-nose doesn't care much for the cage, but what can a sea elephant do when a bunch of humans want him to move in with them? He rests quietly as the cage is lowered onto a truck for the ride to Marineland.

He is getting hungry. Where is he? The funny little animals seem to be treating him well, but Cyra-nose hears strange sounds. The little animals don't snort, he can't hear the waves, and even the hot sun is gone.

Now what? One end of the cage dips into the water of a large pool, and Cyra-nose explores a new home. It feels like ocean water, and it tastes salty, but it certainly is a small ocean.

What a way to eat! Cyra-nose pokes his neck out of the pool and catches a fish without even trying. A young cow from home shares his pool at first. She had better not get in his way at lunchtime.

The men who work with Cyra-nose are trainers. They named their sea elephant Cyra-nose because he reminded them of a famous man called Cyrano. He *also* had a very big nose.

Cyra-nose tries to figure it all out. Above the pool he sees other two-legged animals looking at him. He swims to the bottom and finds some more fish thrown in just for him. Now, if he could only find the beach . . .

Later Cyra-nose looks over a fence next to a new pool where he will live. When a sea elephant pokes his nose at you, stand back! He might lift his head and honk like an automobile horn. Now Cyra-nose feels better about Marineland. The other animals seem friendly. Maybe he won't have to bite any of them.

Cyra-nose has no worries about food at Marineland. All he has to do is open his big mouth, and a trainer hands him a fish. Not bad at all! Cyra-nose soon eats 75 pounds of fish a day, and without moving a flipper.

Even a big bull could get lazy with such an easy life. As Cyra-nose floats, he blows air from his long nose, and splashes water all over the place.

Wait a minute! Cyra-nose finds there's a catch to getting all that free food. The trainer wants him to work. He talks to the animal gently, and gives him hand signals or blows a whistle. The beautiful beast from Guadalupe Island tries to do what he's told. After all, a little work means a lot of fish. Cyra-nose even stands on his back flippers to please the trainer.

After two months at Marineland, Cyra-nose and the trainer are good friends. Why not let the trainer ride on his back? He's not very big.

When Cyra-nose raises his head and tail at the same time, the trainer is very happy. Doing his work well means extra fish for the big bull. That's better than money any day.

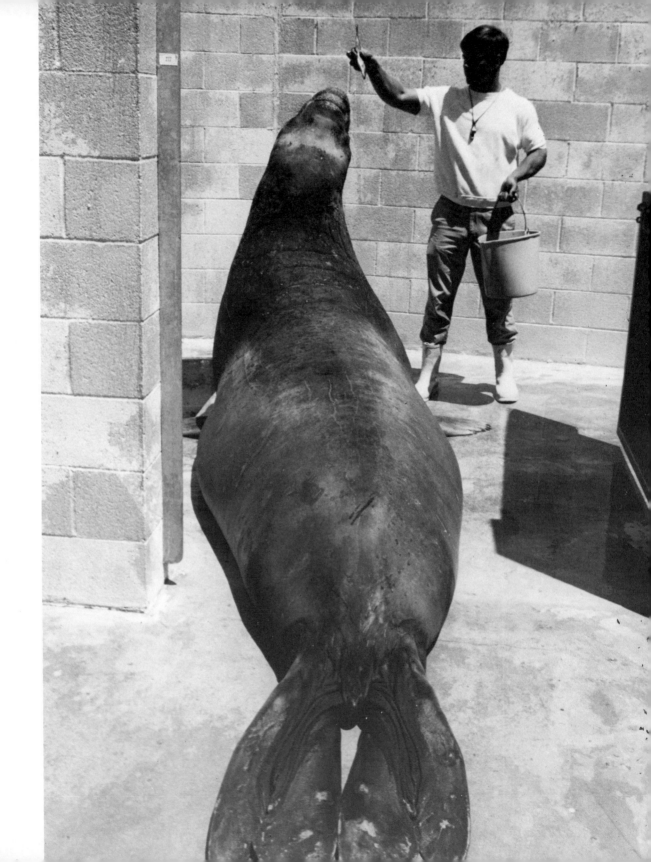

Cyra-nose doesn't know he looks like a blimp with flippers as he follows the trainer to the pool and falls in. The beautiful beast doesn't mind work now, because Marineland is a nice place to live. And the little two-legged animals pet him with their flippers for doing things he used to do for fun on the beach.

Cyra-nose has learned to perform on a Marineland stage where boys and girls watch him. In his first show he does all his tricks well. He barks loudly as he curls his head and tail into a hoop.

Cyra-nose wants to follow the trainer because he has all those fish. But the show isn't over, so Cyra-nose has to stay on the stage.

The trainer in a white coat pretends he is a doctor listening to Cyra-nose's heart. The huge elephant seal shows off in a way that once scared other bulls away.

Cyra-nose lets the trainer stand on his back and pet his nose. The smaller animal seems to have learned his work well, but is he also paid in fish? Cyra-nose doesn't care, as long as he gets plenty of food for playing along in this act. It's easy, compared to swimming all over the ocean looking for a meal.

Cyra-nose gets a hug that feels good. He also likes the sound of people clapping when he performs. What ever happened to Guadalupe Island? Oh well, who cares!

The show is over and Cyra-nose shakes flippers with the trainer. All he has to do is twist, turn or roll. Then he can lie around his pool. How lucky can a sea elephant get? He even has his picture in the newspaper, and it didn't cost him a *mackerel!*

Cyra-nose might live to be 20 years old at Marineland, if he isn't sent back to the Pacific for getting lazy. But work is really play, and the ocean is not far away.

Now really, don't you think he's beautiful? Well, his mother would think so. She'd be happy to know Cyra-nose has a steady job, and is now the most famous sea elephant in Los Angeles!

Glossary

blubber   a layer of fat under a sea animal's skin that keeps it warm in very cold weather or water

bull   the male of certain animals such as cattle and sea elephants

calf   a young animal in families such as the elephant seal, whale or cattle

cow   the female of certain animals such as the elephant seal, whale or seal

elephant seal   the largest animal in the seal family which has a big, curving nose; also called the sea elephant

flipper   a wide, flat paddle which some sea animals have instead of arms or legs—Sea elephants, seals, whales and dolphins can swim fast using their flippers.

harem   a group of female animals that are led by, and mated to, one male

mackerel   a fast-swimming fish of the sea

nurse   to give mother's milk to a young animal; or when a young animal takes milk from its mother

pup   a young seal or sea elephant

sea elephant   another name for elephant seal—the sea animal that has a long nose like an elephant's trunk

tusks   a pair of very long teeth that grow from the mouths of sea elephants, walruses and elephants

G73-17590   j599.7
                                J

Jacobs, Lou
    Cyra-Nose, the sea
    elephant.

-J